WHEN LOVE, HATE, PLEASURE & PAIN COLLIDE

WHEN LOVE, HATE, PLEASURE & PAIN COLLIDE

LYRICAL PHOENIX

CHAPTER 1

When
Love, Hate, Pleasure,
& Pain
Collide
Lyrical Phoenix

CHAPTER 2

Life throws you various ups and downs but it's up to you whether to take it one day at a time or let it take you....

CHAPTER 3

A Letter to Self

Crying sad tears through laughing eyes, is the greatest mystery an unseen surprise, take a break time to realize, beyond the guesstimation of where fate lies, unanswered questions with untruthful replies, plotting your own demise, with unspoken thoughts of suicide, calm on the outside but exploding on the inside.

Dear Heart,

Dear heart you have indeed been broken a time or two,

No other body part knows real pain like you do,

When eyes read lying lips you heard words that were true,

When the mind processed thoughts that shattered you to pieces you picked up those pieces and put them back together without the need of glue.

Dear Eyes,

Dear eyes you have seen things the ears couldn't process,

Looked past defeat to the land of success,

You have seen hurtful things that's caused the mind stress,

You know what it truly feels like to look at a new day and say yes I'm blessed.

Dear Ears,

Dear ears you have heard lies upon lies,

Heard the sounds of inner cries,

Listened to the essence of time as it continuously flies,

Processed emotions hidden between words without stopping to re-
alize.
Dear Mind,
Dear mind you have processed mean and hurtful thoughts,
Continuously replayed scenes dealing with flaws and faults,
Stayed awake through sleepless nights,
Replayed arguments and pointless fights
Dear Hand and Fingers,
Dear hand and fingers you have felt things with only the swiftest bit
of touch or the slightest bit of feel,
Determined if the objects set before you were indeed real,
Opened invisible doorways without even breaking a seal.
Dear Legs and Feet,
Dear legs and feet you have traveled great distances,
Bringing unforeseen paths into existence,
Travelled alone without a complaint in sight just for instance,

A WOMAN LIKE ME

Close your eyes make a wish,
Have you ever had a night begin like this,
But ended like that,
Have you ever been taken to ecstasy and didn't want to come back,
Have you ever had someone freeze time,
Just to use it to blow your mind,
Have you ever felt like life's greatest treasure,
While crossing that thin line between pain and pleasure,
Have you ever felt emotions burst,
While making love so deep it shook the universe,
Have you ever felt like you just couldn't take it,
When an orgasm so good hit you so hard there was no way you could
fake it,
Have you ever had a feeling of pure bliss,

As lips so soft steals your breathe with just a simple kiss,
Have you ever had someone to love you completely,
If not.....you have never had a woman like me.

REAL LIFE

This is real life so no need to yell action, for every consequence there is a chain reaction, cause and effect effect and cause, when you achieve a goal there is no applause, this road you walk is a one way street, walk lookin up and not down at your feet, nor don't look behind at what was or could have been, if you wanna make a change start from within.....

LOVE SCENE

Using pleasure to take away the pain so I cannot feel,
Feeling pure ecstasy is an added bonus in this sex appeal,
Ain't no shame in my game,
Have you moaning whispering my name,
Get rough with me I shall not break,
True love is what I'm giving all you have to do is take,
There's no end let's take it to the extreme,
No lights or cameras just action when you're apart of this love scene

THE UNEXPECTED

Shh let silence fall among us,
There are no words needed now,
There's a right and a wrong way let me show you how,
Let me be your guide just rely on trust,
Without trust what else is there,
The absence of, is like breathing without air,
Gentle caresses leaving eyes with a blank stare,

You for me, me for you that's all that counts at this moment in time,
Put your hand right here notice how your heartbeat reflects mine,
As you start to speak a finger is placed on your lips,
Soft music starts playing soon as we begin the sway our hips,
Candles lit, sigh what could be better than this,
Time stands still as we both lean in for that soft sensual kiss,
Hopes and dreams connected with the slightest interaction,
Take my hand as I lead you on a journey filled with romance and
blissful passion,
Showing how deep love can go when two souls are connected,
Arrive at a destination of pure ecstasy when you encounter the un-
expected.

TELL ME

Tell me you love me with a feeling so right,
Promise to never leave me while holding me so gentle and tight,
Caress my body and allow me to caress yours throughout the night,
Whispering words I long to hear,
Touching my soul but entering through the ear,
Conquer my thoughts leaving not one trace of fear,
Even though we are apart we still remain near,
Stare into my eyes,
While parting my inner thighs,
Pleasuring my body listening to silent cries
The time has come to either sink, swim, or float,
From parted lips escapes a moan that was once caught in the throat,
Enjoying each other presence without the need for applaud, brag,
boast, or gloat

LETTING GO

It took some time

But in my heart you no longer dwell
Living out this dream
In a passionate scene
But nothing is as it seem
Snap back to reality
This feeling's just an epitome
But it's trying to be
What's really true to me
Erasing doubts and fears
Falling upon deaf ears
Blinding eyes
As time flies
Realizing real lies
Find a place and hideaway
It was a waste of time instead
Now I gotta get you out of my head
Time wasted seems like a drastic ending
But it leaves room for open doors of a beautiful new beginning.

PAST LIFE

She's a gun slinging enemy
A mastermind of felonies
She continually escapes this single cell jail in me
Just to empty her shells in me
Then think it's compelling me
Instead it tends to keep repelling me
But I snap back
From this cat nap
And I pack that
In my back pack
And I keep riding
As though it ain't dying

Getting stopped as it hit the curb
I can't see it from your actions
But it reflects in my reactions
From the L's you keep passing
That this is just a fucking word
That goes unheard
Made up of four letters portrayed as a verb.

NAMELESS

Seems like we have known each other forever but it's only been some years,
You cleared all my doubts away and erased a lot of my fears,
Shared with me my smiles and guided me through my tears,
To me you are the world but to the world you are one and that's shameless,
Even though to me you are not faceless but to the world you shall remain nameless...
Dreams becoming realities as we speak,
The heart is a dangerous place that you choose to seek,
Seeing through my eyes far beyond the depths of my soul,
Love is a thing of beauty only with age does one grow old,
Love is timeless,
Finding the right one is priceless,
Soon the time will come when you will no longer be nameless.
Gone is the pain, like the flow of rain down the widow pane, boundariless thoughts no longer driving one insane, no more shadows clouding the membrane,
Love flowing free,
Like the waves of the open sea,
Bonding/binding you to me,
Whispering words caressing bodies emotions flowing deeply,
Making a love that will last,

Never forgetting but choosing to overlook the past,

BROKEN HEARTED

Sometimes it's so hard to say our goodbyes,
Just reflecting on memories past brings tears to my eyes,
I find myself asking why,
Even though I know you would want me to be strong I still can't help but to cry,
But now you are in a better place and pain free,
Now I can say I have a guardian angel forever watching over me,
Our time here is uncertain but until the day we meet again these words are the ones I hold true,
I'll always love and miss you.

SO PASSIONATE

Staring into your pretty brown eyes,
As I crawl between your thighs,
Emotions are not the only thing on the rise,
Falling victim to my prey,
I'm willing to compromise,
Your wish is the command that I shall obey,
Allowing reality to come from a fantasy,
Thoughts relaxing in ecstasy,
Controlling our destiny,
Two becoming one while you're laying with me,
When our legs are intertwined,
Whispers of unspoken words becoming sublime,
Passionate endless tender kisses,
Living in the moment never wanting to forget this,
Making love so intense it's bound to be endless,
Letting the inevitable take hold,

Hormones spinning like a whirlwind,
I'm starting to loose control,
Hearts beating in rhythm without an end.

BALANCE

When you change who you are to be what others want you to be you loose sight of your true self which leaves you blind to reality, with a confused mentality, starring at the mirror searching for oneness but instead finding duality, that's clearly unorthodox, in a self created paradox, your thoughts shall dwell, trying to balance the good and bad traits of life on a libra scale

PHOENIX

Out of the ashes you shall rise,
Peaking through like a new sunrise,
Seems as if it's the first time you're opening your eyes,
Only to realize,
The sight of real lies,
With a full understanding,
There's no need to compromise,
Time is of the essence no use in demanding,
Overcoming the shadowy ashes of bridges long since burned,
Unspoken whispers leaves endless situations as lessons learned,
Thoughts kept hidden leaves a penny saved and another one earned,
Blank starring eyes,
Leaves no room for surprise,
Facing the music before it's too late to realize,
Dwelling in depression is classified as unhealthy,
Refusing to let emotions flow as another unchained melody,

WHAT IS A SOULMATE

What is a soulmate? Hmm a question I choose to ponder, that makes me wonder, if it's what God put together let no man put asunder, that one person you want to be with until you're old, sharing a connection that goes as deep as the soul, feeling oh so right it can't go wrong, makes time stand still so it always feel brand new and young, the true meaning of make it last forever, though you're apart you're separated never.

What is a soulmate? A question I'm asking a second time, reliving that day you called that person mine, or should I say yours, everyday is a new chance for exploration, like opening unexpected doors, not knowing but prepared for an awesome destination, can't explain it because it's felt so deeply, a constant state of ecstasy, is that what you mean to me.

What is a soulmate? Third time's a charm, to this question I have an answer that's not in general, even tho you make me melt inside ima try to stay true to form, allow me to express it but do it lyrical, it's that ONE person I deem to be the rarest of the rare, that ONE person that's always somehow there, providing good love, understanding, honesty, peace, and intense care, in a crowded room but I'm only seeing that ONE, bodily separated but never feeling alone, that ONE in a million, billion, trillion, gladly accepting you for the person you are, or as I am despite flaws or faults, a constant occupant of my dearest deepest loving thoughts, feeling so near despite your physical presence being so far, the real meaning of being loyal always remaining true, so what is a soulmate, well to me that is YOU.

NO LOVE GREATER

Never been a hater just a mind manipulator
a standing ovation giving congratulator
letting my silence teach life long lessons like a mindless educator
doing what I do uniquely never once a duplicator
using my actions to over power your words proving to be such a great
debater being true to yourself there's no love greater

LIFE GOES ON

Life goes on,
You win some you loose some, without realizing you just lost one,
Treated like a child but age wise you are grown,
Standing in the middle of a crowded room yet you still feel alone,
Walking down a bright sunny road but in your eyes its dark and gloomy without the smallest bit of light,
Life is a battle you been gave up the fight,
Nothing to loose and nothing to gain,
Nothing to pay when there is nothing to earn,
Trying to cross over bridges burned,
Another lesson learned,
Sad depressing ways,
 Leaves no room for smile filled days,
Don't feel like staying or going continuously asking why,
Time heals all wounds they say,
Pain is deep but pride is deeper and won't let you cry,
The wounds of time is the price you pay,
When all else fails there is no other way,
Take it all in hide it with a smile and move on,
Even without you wanting it to, indeed life goes on.

CAN YOU

Can you make me scream when you go downtown,
TKO after the countdown can you go another round,
You loving the way I do what I do,
Trying to hold back a moan when I start grinding on you,
Can you outlast me while I put it on you right,
What started during the day can last all night,
There is no way you can miss this flow,
When I take my time do it slow,
Baby can I is the question,

A smile on your face is a welcomed expression,
Can you hear that my heart beat matches your tone,
Whispering your name in the mist of a moan,
I got walls built up can you tear them down,
Experiencing pleasurable pain by the sight of a frown,
More and more is all the neighbors are hearing,
The end of time is the only thing we are fearing,
We about to take a crash course to ecstasy,
With feelings like these, that is our only destiny,
Or should I say destination,
Two plus two equals one after you do some subtraction and dividing
to form this equation.

SEDUCTION

Picture this hands sliding past the stomach coming to a rest upon
thighs,
while time becomes lost starring deeply into eyes,
touching lips sharing a sweet passionate kiss,
closed eyes enjoying this feeling of pure seductive bliss,
putting the mind in a trance,
as tongues perform their own slow dance
Moving to the beat of the rain against the window pane,
final destination is ecstasy the drive is insane,
inside the throat breathe becomes caught,
oh my God what have I gotten myself into is the only thought,
shared emotions on the rise run deep,
after something so intense drifting off into a coma like sleep
Awaking suddenly kissing softly taking the breathe away,
making time freeze as to not forget this day,
taming inhibitions with determination and gift of persuasion,
making a river flow the tongue is the destination,
erotic feels leaving a lasting sensation

THE SILENT PRAYER

As I lay it down preparing to sleep,
I pray in my lungs my breathe will keep,
If I shall die before I wake,
I pray you receive the last breathe I take,
When leaving it all behind is a must,
I pray you understand that it's only my body that's returning to dust,
Have no doubts worries or fear,
I pray you know that even if I'm gone I'm always near,
If the time has come that you no longer can see me,
I pray that you will still feel my presence deeply and internally,
At times you may feel as the tears will never end,
I pray memories bring you peace until we meet again.

UNTITLED

I love you for who you are not just for who you ain't,
emotionally I'm right there with you even when my body can't,
then now forever and still,
more than words can say but I know no one else never will,
open arms accepting flaws and all,
lay your burdens and problems on me no matter how big or small,
this is where I'll gladly stay,
thoughts clinging to memories of you never once going astray,
a lifetime of laughter and passion even an eternity would be too soon,
with me directions are endlessly unknown like floating past the moon